MW00892224

S.O.A.P. BIBLE STUDY METHOD

SCRIPTURE

Always begin your bible study with prayer, asking God to help you understand His Word. Read, and then write down the bible verse or passage of scripture you want to study. It's a good idea to read the scripture out loud when copying it, so that you "hear" the Word. If you do not have enough room to copy the whole passage, you can simply copy the reference (ex. Psalm 23).

OBSERVATION

What does this scripture say? Examine the text by asking the questions: who, what, when, where, why, and how. Context rules, so you often need to read verses before and after your text in order to come to the correct interpretation (what does it mean) of the scripture. Look for key words and/or phrases. If something is repeated, it is important! There are online resources listed on the following page to aid you in observing and interpreting the Word of God.

APPLICATION

How can I apply this scripture in my life? Meditate on what you have learned, asking yourself the following questions. Did God give me any commands I need to obey? Did He show me any sins I need to confess? Did He give me any promises I can claim? How will this scripture help me today? How can this scripture help me in the future? Write down your answers as the Lord speaks to you.

PRAYER

God has spoken, and now it is your turn! Pray His Word back to Him, asking Him to help you apply it to your life. Pray that it will take root and dwell richly in your heart and mind, teaching and correcting you, so that you become more like Jesus. Praise Him because He is good. Thank Him for His grace and help in your times of need, and for everything.

HELPFUL BIBLE STUDY RESOURCES

Bible Study starts with a good Bible. There are many Bible translations, but unfortunately, they are not all equal to each other. Some are no more than a paraphrase, such as The Living Bible and The Message Bible. Others are not the best translations from the original texts, often changing, adding or taking away words and phrases. Since most of us do not read the original languages the Bible was written in, Hebrew and Koine Greek, we need to use a translation that is as close to the original texts as possible. We recommend the New American Standard (NASB), King James Version (KJV), or the New King James Version (NJKV). There are online Bibles, such as **biblehub.com**, where you can read from different versions at the same time for a comparison. You can read more on the topic of translations, and their pros and cons, at the web address below.
https://www.biblesociety.org.uk/explore-the-bible/which-is-the-best-bible-translation/

To accurately observe the scripture, and in order to interpret it, we need to make sure we understand what the key words actually mean. That is, we have to know the real meanings of the words when they were originally written. Words can change meaning over time, but the words in the Bible do not. What it meant when it was written is still what it means today. Knowing the original Hebrew or Greek word and it's meaning, will give you a deeper understanding of the scripture. My favorite Bible study resource for this is the Touch Bible App. This App uses Strong's Concordance, and has the key words already highlighted. You simply touch the highlighted word and you are given the actual word used in the original language and its definitions. This is very helpful because you can have two words in the same verse or passage translated as the same word (ex. "leadeth" in Psalm 23), but it is actually completely different words with different meanings. Knowing this will lead you to a different interpretation and thus, a deeper understanding of the scriptures. Alternatively, you can access Strong's Exhaustive Concordance online at the web address below.
https://www.biblestudytools.com/concordances/strongs-exhaustive-concordance/

The Webster's 1828 Dictionary is an extremely helpful aid in understanding words no longer in common use (as often found in the bible) or words that have changed significantly over the years. If you will be using the KJV of the Bible, you will find this dictionary an indispensible tool. You can access it online at the web addresses below.
http://webstersdictionary1828.com/

Bible Study Guide

Date:___ / ___ / ___

Scripture

_____

_____

_____

Observation

_____

_____

_____

Application

_____

_____

_____

Prayer

_____

_____

_____

Bible Study Guide

Date:___ / ___ / ___

Scripture
_____
_____
_____
_____

Observation
_____
_____
_____
_____

Application
_____
_____
_____
_____

Prayer
_____
_____
_____
_____

Bible Study Guide

Date:___ / ___ / ___

Scripture _____

_____

_____

Observation _____

_____

_____

_____

Application _____

_____

_____

_____

Prayer _____

_____

_____

_____

Bible Study Guide

Date:___ / ___ / ___

Scripture
_____
_____
_____
_____

Observation
_____
_____
_____
_____

Application
_____
_____
_____
_____

Prayer
_____
_____
_____
_____

Bible Study Guide

Date:___ / ___ / ___

Scripture
_____

_____

_____

Observation
_____

_____

_____

_____

Application
_____

_____

_____

_____

Prayer
_____

_____

_____

_____

Bible Study Guide

Date:___ / ___ / ___

Scripture
_____

_____

_____

_____

Observation
_____

_____

_____

_____

Application
_____

_____

_____

_____

Prayer
_____

_____

_____

_____

Bible Study Guide

Date:___ / ___ / ___

Scripture
_____

_____
_____
_____

Observation
_____

_____
_____
_____

Application
_____

_____
_____
_____

Prayer
_____

_____
_____
_____

Bible Study Guide

Date:___ / ___ / ___

Scripture

Observation

Application

Prayer

Bible Study Guide

Date:___ / ___ / ___

Scripture

_____

_____

_____

Observation

_____

_____

_____

_____

Application

_____

_____

_____

_____

Prayer

_____

_____

_____

_____

Bible Study Guide

Date:___ / ___ / ___

Scripture
_____
_____
_____
_____

Observation
_____
_____
_____
_____

Application
_____
_____
_____
_____

Prayer
_____
_____
_____
_____

Bible Study Guide

Date:___ / ___ / ___

Scripture
_____
_____
_____
_____

Observation
_____
_____
_____
_____

Application
_____
_____
_____
_____

Prayer
_____
_____
_____
_____

Bible Study Guide

Date:___ / ___ / ___

Scripture
_____
_____
_____
_____

Observation
_____
_____
_____
_____
_____

Application
_____
_____
_____
_____

Prayer
_____
_____
_____
_____
_____

Bible Study Guide

Date:___ / ___ / ___

Scripture
_____

_____

_____

_____

Observation
_____

_____

_____

_____

Application
_____

_____

_____

_____

Prayer
_____

_____

_____

_____

Bible Study Guide

Date:___ / ___ / ___

Scripture
_____
_____
_____
_____

Observation
_____
_____
_____
_____

Application
_____
_____
_____
_____

Prayer
_____
_____
_____
_____

Bible Study Guide

Date:___ / ___ / ___

Scripture

_____

_____

_____

_____

Observation

_____

_____

_____

_____

Application

_____

_____

_____

_____

Prayer

_____

_____

_____

_____

Bible Study Guide

Date:___ / ___ / ___

Scripture
_____
_____
_____
_____

Observation
_____
_____
_____
_____

Application
_____
_____
_____
_____

Prayer
_____
_____
_____
_____

Bible Study Guide

Date:___ / ___ / ___

Scripture
_____

_____

_____

_____

Observation
_____

_____

_____

_____

Application
_____

_____

_____

_____

Prayer
_____

_____

_____

_____

Bible Study Guide

Date:___ / ___ / ___

Scripture
_____
_____
_____
_____

Observation
_____
_____
_____
_____

Application
_____
_____
_____
_____

Prayer
_____
_____
_____
_____

Bible Study Guide

Date:____ / ____ / ____

Scripture
_____
_____
_____
_____

Observation
_____
_____
_____
_____

Application
_____
_____
_____
_____

Prayer
_____
_____
_____
_____

Bible Study Guide

Date:___ / ___ / ___

Scripture _____
_____
_____
_____

Observation _____
_____
_____
_____

Application _____
_____
_____
_____

Prayer _____
_____
_____
_____

Bible Study Guide

Date:___ / ___ / ___

Scripture

_____

_____

_____

Observation

_____

_____

_____

Application

_____

_____

_____

Prayer

_____

_____

_____

_____

Bible Study Guide

Date:___ / ___ / ___

Scripture
_____
_____
_____
_____

Observation
_____
_____
_____
_____

Application
_____
_____
_____
_____

Prayer
_____
_____
_____
_____

Bible Study Guide

Date:___ / ___ / ___

Scripture

Observation

Application

Prayer

Bible Study Guide

Date:___ / ___ / ___

Scripture
_____
_____
_____
_____

Observation
_____
_____
_____
_____

Application
_____
_____
_____
_____

Prayer
_____
_____
_____
_____

Bible Study Guide

Date:___ / ___ / ___

Scripture

Observation

Application

Prayer

Bible Study Guide

Date:___ / ___ / ___

Scripture
_____
_____
_____
_____

Observation
_____
_____
_____
_____

Application
_____
_____
_____
_____

Prayer
_____
_____
_____
_____

Bible Study Guide

Date:___ / ___ / ___

Scripture

_____

_____

_____

_____

Observation

_____

_____

_____

_____

Application

_____

_____

_____

_____

Prayer

_____

_____

_____

_____

Bible Study Guide

Date:___ / ___ / ___

Scripture
_____

_____

_____

_____

Observation
_____

_____

_____

_____

Application
_____

_____

_____

_____

Prayer
_____

_____

_____

_____

Bible Study Guide

Date:___ / ___ / ___

Scripture

_____

_____

_____

Observation

_____

_____

_____

Application

_____

_____

_____

Prayer

_____

_____

_____

Bible Study Guide

Date:___ / ___ / ___

Scripture

_____

_____

_____

Observation

_____

_____

_____

_____

Application

_____

_____

_____

_____

Prayer

_____

_____

_____

_____

Bible Study Guide

Date:___ / ___ / ___

Scripture

_____

_____

_____

_____

Observation

_____

_____

_____

_____

Application

_____

_____

_____

_____

Prayer

_____

_____

_____

_____

Bible Study Guide

Date:___ / ___ / ___

Scripture

_____

_____

_____

_____

Observation

_____

_____

_____

_____

Application

_____

_____

_____

_____

Prayer

_____

_____

_____

_____

Bible Study Guide

Date:___ / ___ / ___

Scripture
_____

_____

_____

Observation
_____

_____

_____

Application
_____

_____

_____

Prayer
_____

_____

_____

Bible Study Guide

Date:___ / ___ / ___

Scripture

_____

_____

_____

_____

Observation

_____

_____

_____

_____

Application

_____

_____

_____

_____

Prayer

_____

_____

_____

_____

Bible Study Guide

Date:___ / ___ / ___

Scripture
_____

_____

_____

Observation
_____

_____

_____

Application
_____

_____

_____

Prayer
_____

_____

_____

Bible Study Guide

Date:____ / ____ / ____

Scripture _____

_____

_____

_____

Observation _____

_____

_____

_____

_____

Application _____

_____

_____

_____

_____

Prayer _____

_____

_____

_____

_____

Bible Study Guide

Date:___ / ___ / ___

Scripture

Observation

Application

Prayer

Bible Study Guide

Date:___ / ___ / ___

Scripture
_____
_____
_____
_____

Observation
_____
_____
_____
_____

Application
_____
_____
_____
_____

Prayer
_____
_____
_____
_____

Bible Study Guide

Date:____ / ____ / ____

Scripture
_____
_____
_____
_____

Observation
_____
_____
_____
_____

Application
_____
_____
_____
_____

Prayer
_____
_____
_____
_____

Bible Study Guide

Date:___ / ___ / ___

Scripture

_____

_____

_____

_____

Observation

_____

_____

_____

_____

Application

_____

_____

_____

_____

Prayer

_____

_____

_____

_____

Bible Study Guide

Date:___ / ___ / ___

Scripture _____

_____

_____

_____

Observation _____

_____

_____

_____

Application _____

_____

_____

_____

Prayer _____

_____

_____

_____

Bible Study Guide

Date:___ / ___ / ___

Scripture

Observation

Application

Prayer

Bible Study Guide

Date:____ / ____ / ____

Scripture

_____

_____

_____

_____

Observation

_____

_____

_____

_____

Application

_____

_____

_____

_____

Prayer

_____

_____

_____

_____

Bible Study Guide

Date:___ / ___ / ___

Scripture

_____

_____

_____

_____

Observation

_____

_____

_____

_____

Application

_____

_____

_____

_____

Prayer

_____

_____

_____

_____

Bible Study Guide

Date:___ / ___ / ___

Scripture

_____

_____

_____

_____

Observation

_____

_____

_____

_____

Application

_____

_____

_____

_____

Prayer

_____

_____

_____

_____

Bible Study Guide

Date:___ / ___ / ___

Scripture

Observation

Application

Prayer

Bible Study Guide

Date:___ / ___ / ___

Scripture

_____

_____

_____

_____

Observation

_____

_____

_____

_____

Application

_____

_____

_____

_____

Prayer

_____

_____

_____

_____

Bible Study Guide

Date:___ / ___ / ___

Scripture

_____

_____

_____

_____

Observation

_____

_____

_____

_____

Application

_____

_____

_____

_____

Prayer

_____

_____

_____

_____

Bible Study Guide

Date:____ / ____ / ____

Scripture _____

_____

_____

_____

Observation _____

_____

_____

_____

Application _____

_____

_____

_____

Prayer _____

_____

_____

_____

Bible Study Guide

Date:___ / ___ / ___

Scripture
_____
_____
_____
_____

Observation
_____
_____
_____
_____

Application
_____
_____
_____
_____

Prayer
_____
_____
_____
_____

Bible Study Guide

Date:____ / ____ / ____

Scripture
_____

_____

_____

Observation
_____

_____

_____

_____

Application
_____

_____

_____

_____

Prayer
_____

_____

_____

_____

Bible Study Guide

Date:___ / ___ / ___

Scripture

_____

_____

_____

_____

Observation

_____

_____

_____

_____

Application

_____

_____

_____

_____

Prayer

_____

_____

_____

_____

Bible Study Guide

Date:___ / ___ / ___

Scripture

_____

_____

_____

_____

Observation

_____

_____

_____

_____

Application

_____

_____

_____

_____

Prayer

_____

_____

_____

_____

Bible Study Guide

Date:___ / ___ / ___

Scripture
_____
_____
_____
_____

Observation
_____
_____
_____
_____

Application
_____
_____
_____
_____

Prayer
_____
_____
_____
_____

Bible Study Guide

Date:___ / ___ / ___

Scripture

_____

_____

_____

_____

Observation

_____

_____

_____

_____

Application

_____

_____

_____

_____

Prayer

_____

_____

_____

_____

Bible Study Guide

Date:___ / ___ / ___

Scripture
_____
_____
_____
_____

Observation
_____
_____
_____
_____

Application
_____
_____
_____
_____

Prayer
_____
_____
_____
_____

Bible Study Guide

Date:____ / ____ / ____

Scripture

_____

_____

_____

_____

Observation

_____

_____

_____

_____

Application

_____

_____

_____

_____

Prayer

_____

_____

_____

_____

Bible Study Guide

Date:___ / ___ / ___

Scripture

_____

_____

_____

_____

Observation

_____

_____

_____

_____

Application

_____

_____

_____

_____

Prayer

_____

_____

_____

_____

Bible Study Guide

Date:___ / ___ / ___

Scripture
_____

_____

_____

_____

Observation
_____

_____

_____

_____

Application
_____

_____

_____

_____

Prayer
_____

_____

_____

_____

Bible Study Guide

Date:___ / ___ / ___

Scripture

Observation

Application

Prayer

Bible Study Guide

Date:___ / ___ / ___

Scripture
_____

_____

_____

Observation
_____

_____

_____

_____

Application
_____

_____

_____

_____

Prayer
_____

_____

_____

_____

Bibile Study Guide

Date:___ / ___ / ___

Scripture
_____
_____
_____
_____

Observation
_____
_____
_____
_____

Application
_____
_____
_____
_____

Prayer
_____
_____
_____
_____

Bible Study Guide

Date:___ / ___ / ___

Scripture

Observation

Application

Prayer

Bible Study Guide

Date:___ / ___ / ___

Scripture
_____
_____
_____
_____

Observation
_____
_____
_____
_____

Application
_____
_____
_____
_____

Prayer
_____
_____
_____
_____

Bible Study Guide

Date:___ / ___ / ___

Scripture

_____

_____

_____

_____

Observation

_____

_____

_____

_____

Application

_____

_____

_____

_____

Prayer

_____

_____

_____

_____

Bible Study Guide

Date:___ / ___ / ___

Scripture

_____

_____

_____

_____

Observation

_____

_____

_____

_____

Application

_____

_____

_____

_____

Prayer

_____

_____

_____

_____

Bible Study Guide

Date:___ / ___ / ___

Scripture

_____

_____

_____

Observation

_____

_____

_____

Application

_____

_____

_____

Prayer

_____

_____

_____

_____

Bible Study Guide

Date:___ / ___ / ___

Scripture
_____
_____
_____
_____

Observation
_____
_____
_____
_____

Application
_____
_____
_____
_____

Prayer
_____
_____
_____
_____

Bible Study Guide

Date:___ / ___ / ___

Scripture
_____
_____
_____
_____

Observation
_____
_____
_____
_____

Application
_____
_____
_____
_____

Prayer
_____
_____
_____
_____

Bible Study Guide

Date:___ / ___ / ___

Scripture

_____

_____

_____

_____

Observation

_____

_____

_____

_____

Application

_____

_____

_____

_____

Prayer

_____

_____

_____

_____

Bible Study Guide

Date:___ / ___ / ___

Scripture

Observation

Application

Prayer

Bible Study Guide

Date:____/____/____

Scripture

_____

_____

_____

_____

Observation

_____

_____

_____

_____

Application

_____

_____

_____

_____

Prayer

_____

_____

_____

_____

Bible Study Guide

Date:___ / ___ / ___

Scripture
_____

_____

_____

_____

Observation
_____

_____

_____

_____

Application
_____

_____

_____

_____

Prayer
_____

_____

_____

_____

Bible Study Guide

Date:___ / ___ / ___

Scripture

Observation

Application

Prayer

Bible Study Guide

Date:___ / ___ / ___

Scripture

Observation

Application

Prayer

Bible Study Guide

Date:___ / ___ / ___

Scripture
_____

_____

_____

_____

Observation
_____

_____

_____

_____

Application
_____

_____

_____

_____

Prayer
_____

_____

_____

_____

Bible Study Guide

Date:____ / ____ / ____

Scripture
_____
_____
_____

Observation
_____
_____
_____
_____

Application
_____
_____
_____
_____

Prayer
_____
_____
_____
_____

Bible Study Guide

Date:___ / ___ / ___

Scripture

Observation

Application

Prayer

Bible Study Guide

Date:___ / ___ / ___

Scripture

_____

_____

_____

Observation

_____

_____

_____

_____

Application

_____

_____

_____

_____

Prayer

_____

_____

_____

_____

Bible Study Guide

Date:___ / ___ / ___

Scripture

_____

_____

_____

_____

Observation

_____

_____

_____

_____

Application

_____

_____

_____

_____

Prayer

_____

_____

_____

_____

Bible Study Guide

Date:___ / ___ / ___

Scripture

Observation

Application

Prayer

Bible Study Guide

Date:___ / ___ / ___

Scripture

_____

_____

_____

_____

Observation

_____

_____

_____

_____

Application

_____

_____

_____

_____

Prayer

_____

_____

_____

_____

Bible Study Guide

Date:____ / ____ / ____

Scripture

_____

_____

_____

_____

Observation

_____

_____

_____

_____

Application

_____

_____

_____

_____

Prayer

_____

_____

_____

_____

Bible Study Guide

Date:___ / ___ / ___

Scripture
_____

_____

_____

_____

Observation
_____

_____

_____

_____

Application
_____

_____

_____

_____

Prayer
_____

_____

_____

_____

Bible Study Guide

Date:___ / ___ / ___

Scripture

Observation

Application

Prayer

Bible Study Guide

Date:___ / ___ / ___

Scripture

_____

_____

_____

_____

Observation

_____

_____

_____

_____

Application

_____

_____

_____

_____

Prayer

_____

_____

_____

_____

Bible Study Guide

Date:____ / ____ / ____

Scripture
_____

_____

_____

Observation
_____

_____

_____

_____

Application
_____

_____

_____

Prayer
_____

_____

_____

_____

Bible Study Guide

Date:___ / ___ / ___

Scripture
_____
_____
_____
_____

Observation
_____
_____
_____
_____

Application
_____
_____
_____
_____

Prayer
_____
_____
_____
_____

Bible Study Guide

Date:___ / ___ / ___

Scripture

Observation

Application

Prayer

Bible Study Guide

Date:___ / ___ / ___

Scripture

_____

_____

_____

_____

Observation

_____

_____

_____

_____

Application

_____

_____

_____

_____

Prayer

_____

_____

_____

_____

Bible Study Guide

Date:___ / ___ / ___

Scripture
_____
_____
_____
_____

Observation
_____
_____
_____
_____

Application
_____
_____
_____
_____

Prayer
_____
_____
_____
_____

Bible Study Guide

Date:___ / ___ / ___

Scripture

_____

_____

_____

_____

Observation

_____

_____

_____

_____

Application

_____

_____

_____

_____

Prayer

_____

_____

_____

_____

Bible Study Guide

Date:___ / ___ / ___

Scripture
_____

_____

_____

Observation
_____

_____

_____

_____

Application
_____

_____

_____

_____

Prayer
_____

_____

_____

_____

Bible Study Guide

Date:___ / ___ / ___

Scripture

_____

_____

_____

_____

Observation

_____

_____

_____

_____

Application

_____

_____

_____

_____

Prayer

_____

_____

_____

_____

Bible Study Guide

Date:___ / ___ / ___

Scripture

_____

_____

_____

Observation

_____

_____

_____

Application

_____

_____

_____

Prayer

_____

_____

_____

Bible Study Guide

Date:___ / ___ / ___

Scripture

_____

_____

_____

_____

Observation

_____

_____

_____

_____

Application

_____

_____

_____

_____

Prayer

_____

_____

_____

_____

Bible Study Guide

Date:___ / ___ / ___

Scripture
_____

_____

_____

_____

Observation
_____

_____

_____

_____

Application
_____

_____

_____

_____

Prayer
_____

_____

_____

_____

Bible Study Guide

Date:___ / ___ / ___

Scripture
_____
_____
_____
_____

Observation
_____
_____
_____
_____

Application
_____
_____
_____
_____

Prayer
_____
_____
_____
_____

Bible Study Guide

Date:____ / ____ / ____

Scripture
_____

_____

_____

Observation
_____

_____

_____

Application
_____

_____

_____

Prayer
_____

_____

_____

Bible Study Guide

Date:___ / ___ / ___

Scripture
_____
_____
_____
_____

Observation
_____
_____
_____
_____

Application
_____
_____
_____
_____

Prayer
_____
_____
_____
_____

Bible Study Guide

Date:___ / ___ / ___

Scripture

Observation

Application

Prayer

Bible Study Guide

Date:___ / ___ / ___

Scripture

_____
_____
_____
_____

Observation

_____
_____
_____
_____

Application

_____
_____
_____
_____

Prayer

_____
_____
_____
_____

Bible Study Guide

Date:___ / ___ / ___

Scripture

Observation

Application

Prayer

Bible Study Guide

Date:___ / ___ / ___

Scripture
_____
_____
_____
_____

Observation
_____
_____
_____
_____

Application
_____
_____
_____
_____

Prayer
_____
_____
_____
_____

Bible Study Guide

Date:___ / ___ / ___

Scripture

_____

_____

_____

_____

Observation

_____

_____

_____

_____

Application

_____

_____

_____

_____

Prayer

_____

_____

_____

_____

Bible Study Guide

Date:___ / ___ / ___

Scripture
_____
_____
_____
_____

Observation
_____
_____
_____
_____

Application
_____
_____
_____
_____

Prayer
_____
_____
_____
_____

Bible Study Guide

Date:___ / ___ / ___

Scripture
_____
_____
_____
_____

Observation
_____
_____
_____
_____

Application
_____
_____
_____
_____

Prayer
_____
_____
_____
_____

Bible Study Guide

Date:___ / ___ / ___

Scripture
_____
_____
_____
_____

Observation
_____
_____
_____
_____

Application
_____
_____
_____
_____

Prayer
_____
_____
_____
_____

Bible Study Guide

Date:___ / ___ / ___

Scripture

Observation

Application

Prayer

Bible Study Guide

Date:___ / ___ / ___

Scripture

_____

_____

_____

_____

Observation

_____

_____

_____

_____

Application

_____

_____

_____

_____

Prayer

_____

_____

_____

_____

_____

Bible Study Guide

Date:___ / ___ / ___

Scripture

_____

_____

_____

Observation

_____

_____

_____

Application

_____

_____

_____

Prayer

_____

_____

_____

Bible Study Guide

Date:___ / ___ / ___

Scripture
_____
_____
_____
_____

Observation
_____
_____
_____
_____

Application
_____
_____
_____
_____

Prayer
_____
_____
_____
_____

For spiral bound journals (personalized and non-personalized) and other products with this and other designs, please visit us at our Etsy shop.
www.nimblemuseprintables.etsy.com

For questions and/or concerns, contact us at
nimblemuse@gmail.com

If you have enjoyed this publication and found it useful, we would be grateful if you would leave us a review.
Thank you.

Made in the USA
Middletown, DE
14 September 2021

48222997R00071